A Note to Parents

DK READERS is a compelling programme for beginning readers, designed in conjunction with leading literacy experts, including Maureen Fernandes, B.Ed (Hons). Maureen has spent many years teaching literacy, both in the classroom and as a consultant in schools.

Beautiful illustrations and superb full-colour photographs combine with engaging, easy-to-read stories and informational texts to offer a fresh approach to each subject in the series. Each DK READER is guaranteed to capture a child's interest while developing his or her reading skills, general knowledge and love of reading.

The five levels of DK READERS are aimed at different reading abilities, enabling you to choose the books that are exactly right for your child:

Pre-level 1: Learning to read

Level 1: Beginning to read

Level 2: Beginning to read alone

Level 3: Reading alone

Level 4: Proficient readers

The 'normal' age at which a child begins to read can be anywhere from three to eight years old. Adult participation through the lower levels is very helpful for providing encouragement, discussing storylines and sounding out unfamiliar words.

No matter which level you select, you can be sure that you are helping your child learn to read, then read to

LONDON, NEW YORK, MUNICH,
MELBOURNE, AND DELHI

For Dorling Kindersley
Senior Editor Alastair Dougall
Editorial Assistant Jo Casey
Designer Owen Bennett
Design Manager Rob Perry
Publishing Manager Simon Beecroft
Category Publisher Alex Allan
Production Controller Amy Bennett
Production Editor Sean Daly

Reading Consultant
Maureen Fernandes

First published in Great Britain in 2009 by
Dorling Kindersley Limited, 80 Strand,
London, WC2R 0RL

09 10 11 12 10 9 8 7 6 5 4 3 2 1
DD529 – 04/09

Published in the USA by DK Publishing

A CIP catalogue record for this book
is available from the British Library

ISBN: 978-1-4053-3900-1

Colour reproduction by Alta Image, UK
Printed and bound by L-Rex, China

Discover more at
www.dk.com

Contents

DK READERS

READING
3
ALONE

JF

AWESOME
POWERS

Written by Michael Teitelbaum

DK

Introduction

Who is Wolverine? He's a powerful mutant. He's a big bad fighting machine with a really nasty attitude. He's loud and aggressive. He's quiet and menacing. He's the ultimate loner, but he's also a great team player.

Above all, Wolverine is a member of the group known as the X-Men. Every member of the X-Men has awesome powers and Wolverine is no exception. Wolverine uses those powers to battle evil mutants and anyone else who intends to do harm to Earth and its people.

Wolverine's razor-sharp claws and amazing mutant abilities make him a fighting machine not to be messed with!

What is a mutant?

All Super Heroes have special powers.
Spider-Man got his powers from the bite
of a radioactive spider. The Hulk got his
powers from a gamma-bomb explosion.

The X-Men
The X-Men are a team of mutants put together by Professor Charles Xavier (Professor X). He is a powerful mutant who can read minds.

But mutants are different. Mutants are born with their special abilities. Like his fellow X-Men, Wolverine is a mutant. Mutants have all kinds of powers. Some mutants can read minds. Others can control the weather. Most mutants look just like humans, but mutants are feared or hated by many humans.

Nightcrawler was chased out of his home by people who feared him.

Healing ability

Wolverine's main mutant power is his amazing healing ability. When a normal human gets injured, the cells in his or her body take a long time to repair themselves. Wolverine can recover from an injury in minutes – even from a knife, sword, or gunshot wound! This ability has also given him a very long life. He's more than 100 years old!

Wolverine has the ability to recover from an injury that would kill a normal person.

Weapon X

A secret Canadian government project, Weapon X, was trying to create a super-soldier. The Weapon X scientists wanted to strengthen a human being's skeleton with the unbreakable metal adamantium. To do this, they needed to find someone capable of surviving the operation.

Agents of Weapon X kidnapped Wolverine. His healing ability enabled him to survive the operation, but his life changed forever.

Brainwashed
Following the operation, Weapon X agents tried to brainwash Wolverine. They hoped he would do whatever they told him to do. But their attempts failed and drove him insane.

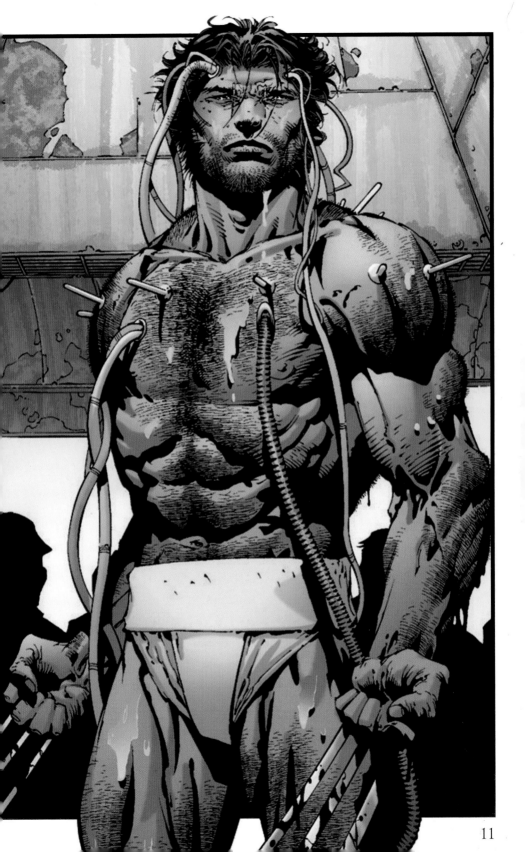

Wolverine's skeleton

Having a skeleton strengthened with adamantium – the hardest known metal on Earth – has transformed Wolverine's life. Wolverine is now virtually indestructible.

Nothing stands in the way of Wolverine!

Adamantium has made his already powerful body incredibly strong. It also makes his bones unbreakable. When Wolverine is attacked, he may get injured, but the adamantium in his body protects his skeleton. It also helps to protect his vital inner organs.

It doesn't take much to make Wolverine angry!

Wolverine's claws

As a mutant, Wolverine was born with claws. Those claws were made from his real bones, and they sprang from his fists during times of stress or danger. The first time they appeared, Wolverine realised he was different from other people. In time, he learnt to control his claws.

Feral Wolverine
When Magneto ripped the adamantium from Wolverine's bones, Wolverine turned into a wild beast.

When Weapon X added adamantium to Wolverine's skeleton, they attached the super-hard metal to his claws as well. Now they are incredibly sharp and powerful. Wolverine's adamantium claws can slice through just about anything.

When Wolverine is in danger, his claws pop out.

Resistance and endurance

Wolverine's mutant healing ability stops him from being harmed by poison. His body is also unaffected by drugs and he is immune to disease.

His amazing powers of endurance enable him to last much longer than a normal human being when doing physical activities, such as running or fighting.

Wolverine's healing ability stops him from getting sick.

He also has increased agility and lightning-quick reflexes. Combined with his strength and healing ability, Wolverine's powers of resistance and endurance make him an almost unbeatable fighting machine.

Namor the Sub-Mariner is no match for Wolverine's mighty strength and agility!

Superhuman senses

During parts of his life, Wolverine lived
in the wild like an animal. Luckily for
him, his mutant powers include
superhuman senses. His enhanced powers
of sight, smell and hearing are more like
those of an animal than a human.

His increased sense of sight allows him to see objects or enemies in the far distance. His amazing hearing helps him hear attackers

approaching from far away, while his sense of smell allows him to identify an object or enemy by scent alone.

Tracker
Wolverine's superhuman senses make him a terrific tracker. He has helped governments, spies and even the X-Men track down criminals in the wild. With Wolverine on your trail, it won't be long before you're caught.

Other abilities

During his long life Wolverine has been a soldier, a C.I.A. agent, a samurai warrior, a spy and a member of the X-Men. Because of his training for all these jobs he has gained skill in many forms of combat.

A motorbike is Wolverine's favourite mode of transport.

Language expert
Wolverine speaks
Japanese, Russian,
Chinese, Cheyenne,
Lakota, Spanish, French,
Thai and Vietnamese.

He is a master of hand-to-hand combat, and skilled in just about every fighting system in the world, including martial arts. He is also an expert with weapons, vehicles, computer systems, and explosives.

All of this knowledge helps make Wolverine's awesome mutant powers that much more awesome.

Wolverine's main weapons are his super-sharp claws.

Who is Wolverine?

So now you know about Wolverine's powers and abilities. But who is this mysterious mutant? His real name is James Howlett. James was the son of wealthy landowners. He grew up on a big estate with rich parents, but he had a difficult childhood.

Logan

When young James Howlett ran away from his home he took the name "Logan" to hide his true identity. Logan was actually the name of the groundskeeper on the Howlett estate.

James's mother was sick for much of his early life and his father didn't pay him much attention. James discovered that he was not like other kids when claws shot out from his hands for the first time. He was terrified of this strange ability and ran away from home.

The first time James's claws popped out was a frightening experience.

Soldier, Samurai, Super Hero

After he left home, James found work in a mining camp. At times he would disappear and live in the wild like an animal. His enhanced senses and mutant powers helped him survive.

Later, he served as a soldier in both World War I and World War II. He then worked as a secret agent for the C.I.A. For a while, he lived in Japan, where he became a samurai warrior.

During his time as a samurai, Wolverine learnt new ways to use his claws .

After the Weapon X project turned him into Wolverine he worked as a Super Hero with Alpha Flight, a team of Canadian heroes.

Alpha Flight

James Hudson was a Canadian secret agent. When he heard about the American Super Hero team called the Fantastic Four, he decided to form a Canadian hero team. He called it Alpha Flight.

Joining the X-Men

Wolverine was asked to be the leader of Alpha Flight. However, around the same time, he met Professor Charles Xavier, leader of the X-Men. Xavier recognised that Wolverine was a mutant, like himself and his students.

Professor X asked Wolverine to join the X-Men. At Professor X's School for Gifted Youngsters, Wolverine found a home at last. He began helping younger mutants learn how to live with their powers.

School for Gifted Youngsters
Some mutants have been attacked because they are so different. Professor X set up his school so mutants could have a safe place to learn to control their powers.

Powers of the X-Men

All of Wolverine's fellow X-Men have amazing mutant powers. Professor X has great mental powers. He can read minds and send messages into the minds of others. He can use his mutant power to paralyse people, erase people's memories, or knock them out with powerful mental bolts.

Jean Grey has mental powers, too. She can read minds and move objects with her thoughts.

Cyclops has a power that is tough to control. Powerful optic blasts shoot from his eyes. He must wear a special visor to hold back these blasts.

Rogue has the ability to fly incredibly fast.

Rogue has the power to absorb people's memories and life energy just by touching them. But her touch can harm the person she touches. If Rogue touches a Super Hero or a mutant, she will absorb that person's super powers.

Nightcrawler can transport himself from one place to another. He vanishes and then, an instant later, he reappears somewhere else.

Storm has the power to control the weather. She can bring hail, fog, rain, snow, or change the temperature of the air, and she can whip up winds of hurricane force.

Storm's eyes glow white when she is using her powers.

Wolverine's enemies

Wolverine has many super-powered enemies. Some of them are mutants. Magneto is one of the most powerful

mutants in the world. He has the power to control magnetism. He has battled Wolverine and the X-Men many times.

Magneto believes that mutants should rule ordinary humans.

Sabretooth has the same mutant healing abilities as Wolverine. While Wolverine works hard to control his animal side, Sabretooth remains a savage beast.

The evil mutant Mystique has the power to shape-shift. She can make herself look like anyone she chooses.

No one knows how old Mystique really is because she can change the way she looks.

Toad lives up to his name. He has superhuman leaping ability, and a long tongue that snaps out and attacks.

Juggernaut is actually Charles Xavier's stepbrother. A magic ruby he found in a cave gave him tremendous strength. Once Juggernaut begins moving in one direction, no force on Earth can stop him.

Juggernaut has amazing power.

Apocalypse is a 5,000-year-old mutant. He can change his shape and form a shield made from a section of his body. Even Wolverine's adamantium claws have trouble slicing through Apocalypse's shields.

Apocalypse can turn his arms into wings or jets.

Wolverine vs. Sabretooth

Sabretooth has the same mutant abilities as Wolverine. He, too, has amazing healing powers and razor-sharp claws. He is more than 100 years old, just like Wolverine.

Wolverine and Sabretooth first battled in the early 1900s. They both loved a young Indian girl called Silver Fox. When Sabretooth saw Wolverine with Silver Fox, he attacked her. Silver Fox's injuries were fatal, and she died.

Weapon X
Like Wolverine, Sabretooth was also used by the Weapon X project. He, too, has had his bones strengthened by adamantium.

Wolverine vs. Sentinel robots

The giant Sentinel robots were created to destroy all mutants. This makes them enemies of Wolverine and his fellow X-Men. These huge, powerful robots have just one thing in mind – to attack and wipe out mutants. Wolverine needs all his cleverness, strength and agility to defeat these enormous metal robots.

Wolverine attacks a Sentinel robot.

Sentinel robots can fire destructive bolts from their hands.

His main battle strategy when fighting
a Sentinel robot is to attack its head with
his claws. His claws can slice right
through the Sentinel's metal heads and
destroy their wiring and programming.

Wolverine vs. Lord Shingen

During the time Wolverine lived in Japan, he fell in love with a woman called Mariko. Mariko's father, Lord Shingen, wanted Wolverine to prove that he was worthy of his daughter and challenged him to a fight.

The two used traditional Japanese swords. Despite all his powers, Wolverine was no match for Shingen in a sword fight.

Mariko was frightened of Wolverine at first, but she soon fell in love with him.

In the middle of the duel
Wolverine popped his claws out. But
Lord Shingen avoided his blows and
defeated Wolverine with his sword.
Wolverine's healing power enabled
him to recover from his wounds.

White King Black Queen Black King White Queen

Wolverine vs. Hellfire Club

To the outside world, the members of the
Hellfire Club are the wealthy and powerful
of high society. But Wolverine and his
fellow X-Men know better. The Hellfire
Club is a front for a group of mutants who
want to control humanity.

Wolverine must use all his powers to battle the mutants of the Hellfire Club. Among their leaders are the White King, Black Queen, Black King and White Queen. The Black King can absorb energy that gives him super strength and speed. The White Queen can place thoughts into other people's minds and control their actions.

The Hellfire Club Soldiers don't stand a chance against Wolverine!

Wolverine vs. Hulk

Wolverine and the Hulk are both incredible fighters. They both have great strength. They are both fueled by rage. They are both very difficult to injure.

Wolverine leaps through the air to take on the mighty Hulk.

They have fought many epic battles. Although Wolverine can recover quickly, he knows that being smashed by the Hulk is no fun at all. He uses his leaping ability and acrobatic skills to stay out of the way of the Hulk's big green fists.

In some of their battles, Wolverine has knocked the Hulk down. But the green giant always gets back up ready to battle again.

Most opponents would be nervous looking up at the Hulk, but not Wolverine!

Awesome powers unleashed

Many mutants and Super Heroes have powers. But few have powers as awesome as Wolverine's. His mutant abilities make him almost indestructible. His animal nature and anger fuel him. The many fighting skills he has learnt allow him to take on any enemy.

Wolverine is not easy to get along with. He doesn't always like being part of a team. But as long as he's fighting on your side, you've got an amazingly powerful ally. Just don't make him mad!

Glossary

aggressive
Pushy, forceful.

agility
The ability to move quickly and precisely.

ally
A friend or helper.

brainwash
To convince someone to do something they don't want to do, or believe something that they really don't believe.

C.I.A.
The Central Intelligence Agency of the US government, concerned with activities involving national security.

endurance
Ability to do something for a long time.

estate
A large house surrounded by land.

immune
Unable to be hurt by.

indestructible
Unbreakable.

juggernaut
An unstoppable force.

loner
One who prefers to spend time alone.

mutant
Someone with an extra ability.

optic
To do with the eyes.

paralyse
Stop from moving.

samurai
A Japanese warrior.

savage
Brutal, violent, uncivilised.

stamina
Ability to keep going.

teleport
Move instantly from one place to another.

transport
Move.

visor
Eye shade.